THE GHOSTLY TALES OF
OF
THE LONG BEACH PENINSULA

Published by Arcadia Children's Books
A Division of Arcadia Publishing
Charleston, SC
www.arcadiapublishing.com

Spooky America is a trademark of Arcadia Publishing, Inc.

First published 2022

Manufactured in the United States

ISBN 978-1-4671-9863-9

Library of Congress Control Number: 2022932230

Notice: The information in this book is true and complete to the best of our knowledge. It is offered without guarantee on the part of the author or Arcadia Publishing. The author and Arcadia Publishing disclaim all liability in connection with the use of this book.

Photo pp. 36, 88 courtesy of Sydney Stevens.
All other images courtesy of Shutterstock.com.

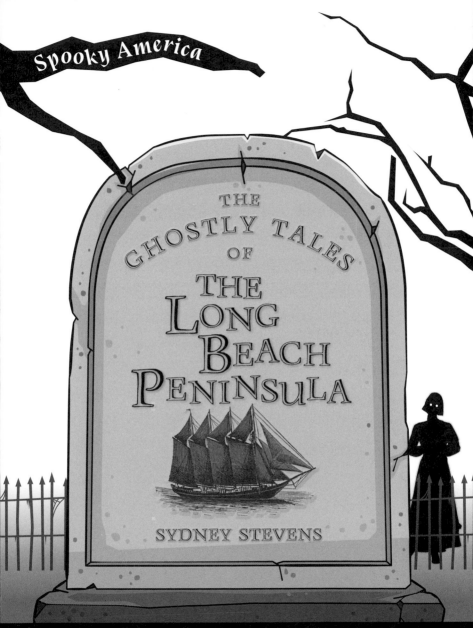

Spooky America

THE
GHOSTLY TALES
OF
THE
LONG
BEACH
PENINSULA

SYDNEY STEVENS

Adapted from *Ghost Stories of the Long Beach Peninsula* by Sydney Stevens

arcadia
CHILDREN'S BOOKS

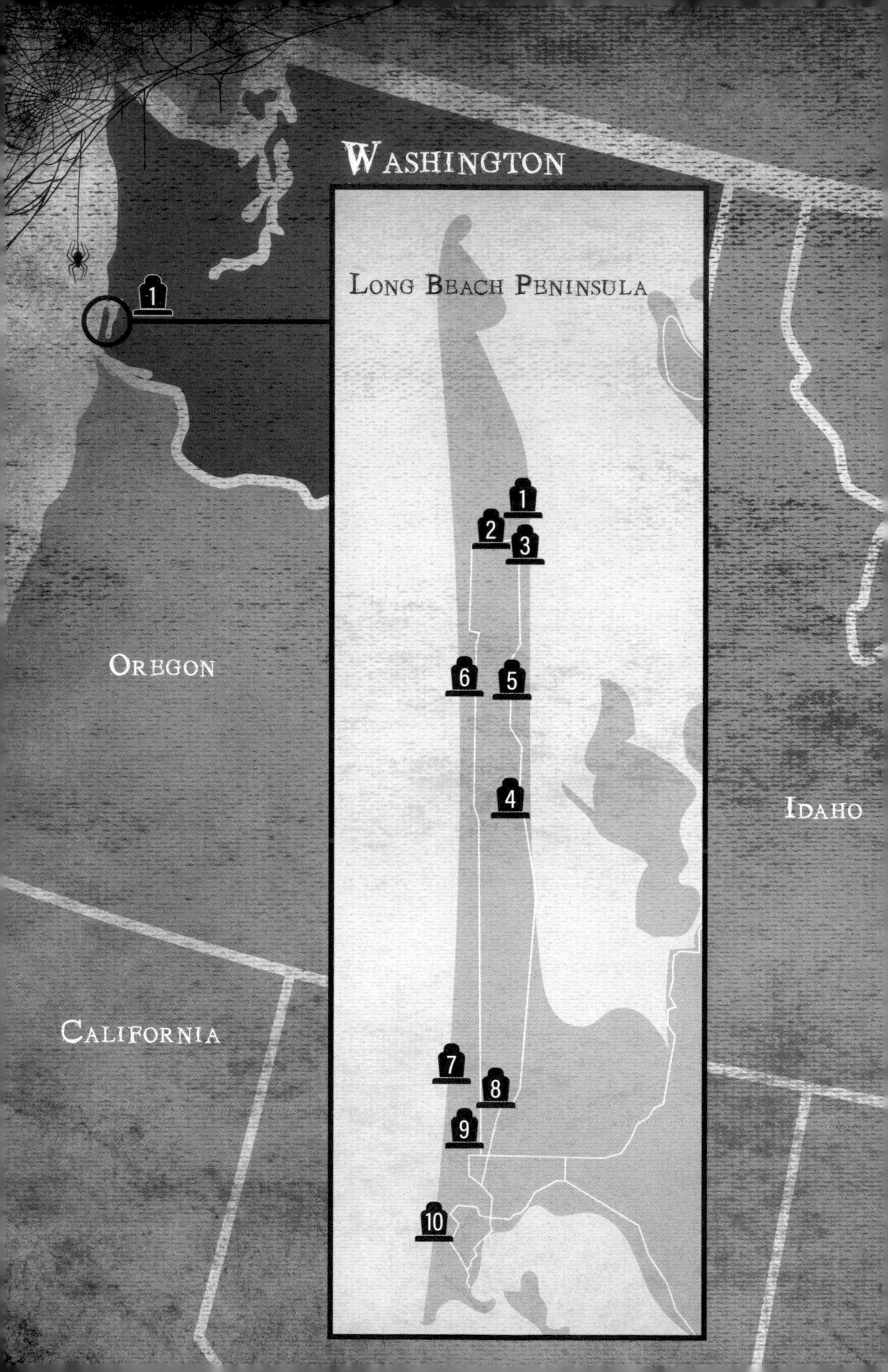

WASHINGTON

LONG BEACH PENINSULA

1

2 1
3

6 5

4

7

8

9

10

OREGON

CALIFORNIA

IDAHO

TABLE OF CONTENTS & MAP KEY

Oysterville Church

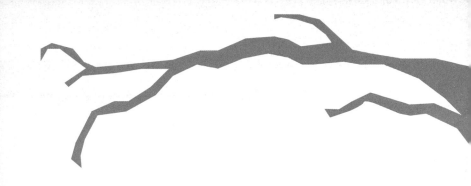

Introduction

The Long Beach Peninsula is a slender finger of sand sitting right on the edge of the continent— a fragile barrier against the crashing waves of the Pacific Ocean and the relentless winds that come from every direction, depending on the season.

Winter is often called "the storytelling season," because the nights are long and dark and rainy in this corner of Washington State. As windows rattle and the old beach houses shudder and shake, it is no wonder that many of the stories are about ghosts—the ghosts of sailors lost at sea or perhaps the spirits of the pioneers who once lived in these same villages and sat around these very fireplaces telling stories of their own.

Even in modern times, the Peninsula is hard to reach. No planes or trains or long-distance buses come here. Not even a ferry boat or a cruise ship. Those who live here tend to have deep roots—their families go back many generations and, often, so do the ghosts. Do the ghosts hang around because they can't find a way off this

remote strip of land? Are the dense forests of spruce and cedar too hard to get through? Or could they be trapped in the nooks and crannies of old, empty buildings? Is that why there are so many of them?

Or do the ghosts, just like the storytellers and their listeners, prefer this out-of-the-way part of the country? Do the ghosts of the Long Beach Peninsula want to be known and talked about? Perhaps you can decide as you read the spooky stories in the pages of this book.

CHAPTER 1

Mrs. Crouch, the Preacher's Wife

It was dark. Very, very dark. No street lights. No moon or stars. And then the noise began.

Tap-tap-tap.

Tap-a-tap-tap-tap. Tap-tap-tap-tap. Tap.

The bedside clock said 2:15. I'd been asleep for almost an hour, and then suddenly that tapping had me wide awake. It was a commonplace sound, not scary, but I couldn't quite place it. And where was it coming from? I was all alone in the big Oysterville house where I had grown up. I was housesitting while my parents were away. And it was the middle of the night. And so dark.

Tap-tap. Tap-tap.

It was nearby. But where?

I turned on the light. The noise stopped. The familiar room with its pink flowered wallpaper and old-fashioned furniture looked as it always had. Here, in "my" room overlooking the old Oysterville Church, the last twenty years seemed to evaporate, and I felt ten years old again.

Finally, I realized the noise was coming

from the next-door bedroom, the one we always thought of as the "littlest kid's room" because it was so small. Bravely, I went to investigate, even though the hair on the back of my neck was standing straight up.

Then I saw it! A typewriter! Of course! But it was the strangest looking typewriter and certainly one I had never seen before. It was from long ago, one of the very first typewriters—way before computers and keyboards, before cell phones and touch screens.

Satisfied, I went back to bed and slept soundly the rest of the night.

At this point in the story, people often ask, "Did you put a piece of paper in the typewriter?"

I wish I had been that clever. But I don't think I could have figured out where to put the paper. This typewriter was definitely from the dark ages.

The other weird thing—while I was certain someone had been typing, I never wondered who it might be, and the idea of a ghost never occurred to me. In fact, once I was satisfied about what that tap-tap-tapping was, I never thought about it again. Not until my parents came home weeks later. When I finally asked my mother about that strange old typewriter, she said she had loaned to the local museum. They had had it for years but had recently returned it. And when I told her about that midnight tapping, she laughed, "Oh, that was probably Mrs. Crouch!"

"Who?" And so my mother "introduced" me to Sarah Crouch, the twenty-one-year-old wife of the first preacher at the Baptist church. Since then, Mrs. C. and I have become very well acquainted, even though she died tragically more than one hundred years ago!

I should say right here and now that I don't believe in ghosts. Not really. Never mind that I've now known Mrs. Crouch for years. And never mind that people I respect and love have had experiences with our ghost. Most of all, never mind that I have had several encounters with her, myself, though I've never actually seen her or heard her voice! I'm not a believer. Not really.

According to my mother, "our" ghost had come to Oysterville in 1892 with her husband, Pastor Josiah Crouch, and their baby daughter.

The house I grew up in was the house the Crouches lived in. It was fifty years since the town's founding, and Oysterville was no longer a boomtown. By then, the little native oysters that had made the town famous were just about gone. Most of the population had moved away, and Oysterville was no longer the most important town in the county.

Josiah Crouch and his family were well liked. The neighbors later said that Mrs. Crouch had a lovely singing voice but that she was very shy. Nevertheless, the next summer, she and the baby went with her husband on a church call up the Willapa River way across the bay from Oysterville. During the visit, there was a terrible accident, and Mrs. Crouch was drowned.

The newspaper said that the family had gone out in a rowboat. Mrs. Crouch had wanted to row the boat, and while she was trading places with her husband, the boat lurched and they were all thrown into the river. Reverend Crouch managed to save himself and the baby, but Mrs. Crouch drowned. It took two hours for neighbors searching the river with long-handled rakes to find her body.

Because Oysterville was far away and transportation difficult, Mrs. Crouch was buried at Fern Hill Cemetery near where she drowned.

But the burial did not put the story of her drowning to rest.

The women who had prepared Mrs. Crouch for burial had seen marks on her neck, and it wasn't long before the people of Oysterville demanded that the body be dug up. But the three doctors who examined the corpse could not determine what had made the marks. They could have been finger marks from the preacher's hands. Or they could have been from the rakes used to recover her body.

Great pressure was put upon the sheriff to arrest Reverend Crouch and bring him to trial. "Let a jury decide!" they demanded. But before the warrant could be served, Crouch took his baby daughter and left town.

Over the years, bits and pieces of information about Josiah Crouch have been found in old church records and tucked away in the attic of this house where I grew up. Like clues in a detective story, they paint a fascinating picture, but in this particular mystery, there are still more questions than answers.

Now that it is my turn to live in the old house, I do keep paper in that peculiar typewriter, still close by the place where I first heard it

tap-tap-tapping. But the keys have remained silent since that dark night so many years ago, even though Mrs. C. does make herself known to me and my family every now and again. So far, she has always been playful, never scary or mean. She especially likes to turn pictures back to front and to open cupboard doors or dresser drawers— apparently for no reason. Or is she looking for something? And . . . just lately we've begun to think that her husband Josiah is hanging around, as well. So far there is no evidence of trouble between them. But stay tuned. You never can tell with ghosts.

yes

A B C D E
N O P Q

5

You Can Call Me Uncle Will

"He told us his name was Will Cox and that he had been killed by a knife. We never could keep sharp knives in the house. They would just disappear," says Jennifer Lonergan of Ocean Park. "He didn't take table knives or butter knives. Just kitchen knives with sharp points and sharp blades. They are the ones that would vanish. Once mom found a missing knife in the garden months after it disappeared. But usually, they never showed up again."

Jennifer was nine or ten years old when Will Cox made himself known. She lived in the Little Red Cottage in Oysterville with her mom and stepdad, Ruby and Pete Heckes.

"The house was small," she told me. "You walked directly into the main room, which was the kitchen-dining-living room area. Straight in front of you was a little hallway with a bedroom on each side and a bathroom in the middle. That was it.

"We had a large glass cabinet right by the front door. I was always a little worried that I would bump into it and damage the keepsakes that were inside. One night, there was a huge crash that woke us all up, and we all rushed into the living room expecting to see that cabinet and its contents totally smashed. Not a thing was broken. Not even disturbed."

That event prompted the family to find out what was going on. They went to the Ouija board for help. (A Ouija board, also known as a spirit board, is a flat board marked with the letters of the alphabet, the numbers 0 through 9, the words "yes" and "no," and occasionally "hello" and "goodbye." It is used to ask questions, which some people believe are answered by the spirits of dead people.)

"That was Pete's idea," Jennifer remembers. "He said that's what spiritualists use to talk to those who have died. And it worked! That's when we found out we had a ghost named Will Cox. According to him, he was taking our knives away to keep me safe! He told me to call him Uncle Will and that he was watching over me. Or at least that was the message he sent on the Ouija board.

"He sent us quite a few messages, but we never did see him, even though I kept asking.

He told me that I wasn't 'ready.' The last time I asked, we were all sitting at the table with the Ouija board and there was a really loud THUMP. I jumped straight out of my chair. 'See I told you that you weren't ready!' he said."

Will Cox stayed in touch with Jennifer's family, even after they had left the Little Red Cottage. "In fact, Jennifer says, "we moved twice before Pete's house on the bay was finished. Through both those moves, Will Cox stuck to us. When we finally moved into the bay house, he stopped bothering us."

So, who was Will Cox? No record exists of a Will Cox, a William Cox, or even a Wilcox ever having lived in Oysterville—not in the census reports and not in the cemetery archives. Nor, as far as any research experts can determine, was there ever anyone on the Peninsula by that name.

The Little Red Cottage is the oldest structure in Oysterville and probably the oldest on the Peninsula, so the building seems a perfect place for a ghost. It was built in 1857 by Joel Munson, a retired sea captain. Helping him were the two Kimball brothers, Byron and Nathan. They had all come to Oysterville to make their fortunes in the booming oyster trade. The Kimball brothers had a very good reason to feel protective toward a child. Just ten years before, when they were eight and ten years old, they and their sisters had survived the 1847 Whitman Massacre at Waiilatpu, near the site of today's Walla Walla. But neither was named Will Cox. Not even close.

Captain Munson left Oysterville in 1863. Two years later, he was appointed lightkeeper at the Cape Disappointment Lighthouse in Ilwaco at the south end of the Peninsula. The following year, the Little Red Cottage became the very first Pacific County Courthouse, and it continued to serve that purpose until a new, two-story courthouse was built two blocks to the north.

From then on, there were many owners and renters of the Little Red Cottage, but only one other tenant ever reported any ghost activity. Ken Driscoll of Ocean Park rented the cottage for a time shortly after the Heckes family left. He later said that he was occasionally visited during the wee hours by someone who would pull the quilts off his bed.

"There would be a struggle," Ken said. "I would tug and he would tug. But there never was anyone to actually see."

Was it the same Will Cox? Taking something that was not rightfully his (like knives from Ruby's kitchen) sounds a bit like Uncle Will's "M.O." Surely, though, removing Ken's covers on cold winter nights couldn't have been considered a good thing. And Ken wasn't a child who needed protecting, even by a ghost.

My uncle, author Willard Espy, owned the cottage for over twenty years—from 1976 to 1997. Neither he nor his wife, Louise, ever told any tales about seeing ghosts or hearing things go bump in the night. Willard was as fond of spooky stories as the next person, and I'm sure if Will Cox had made himself known during those years, the story would have shown up in one of Willard's many books.

As it stands, Will Cox remains a mystery, and the picturesque Little Red Cottage in Oysterville reveals nothing of its spirited past. At least for now, Jennifer and her family are still on the lookout for stories or information about a long ago Oysterville man who was killed with a knife— especially a man who might have been known around town as "Uncle Will."

Ned Osborn,
Jilted Suitor

When I first moved to Oysterville, the old Ned Osborn house was owned by Dolores and Norm Dutchuk. In a village known for its characters, Norm was among the most colorful. In fact, when he died some years later, Dolores had "The Mad Russian of Oysterville" carved on his tombstone. He was "not mad like angry or insane," their son Mike is quick to explain. "More the wild-and-crazy-guy kind of mad."

Norm was a fun-loving people and party person. A salesman in Portland, Oregon, he often gave a getaway to his Oysterville house to his best clients. And during the thirty or forty weekends a year that Norm was at the house, there was often a party going on. If the weather was good, the party was out in the front yard, and Norm's end of the quiet village street could become "a little boisterous."

Norm looked like a character, too. An enthusiastic hunter, he had lost an eye on a pheasant hunting expedition long ago. His one glass eye, though a good color match for his real eye, was a little off center. It gave him a distinctive, somewhat zany appearance.

It was a Sunday after one of his famous parties that I met Norm. He came dashing over to my Uncle Willard Espy's cottage where Willard, his wife, Louise, and I were having coffee out on the deck. "Were we too noisy last night, Willard?" Norm asked.

"Not at all, Norm," Willard answered with a chuckle. "In fact, I thought the party broke up a little earlier than usual."

"Yeah, I had to send them all home. That's what I want to talk to you about. Around midnight or so I went into the house to get another drink and a man I'd never seen before came down the stairs. It was the darndest thing. He said to me 'Get those people out of here. Right now!' And I could tell he meant business. So, I sent everyone home. I was wondering if you had any idea who that man was."

Willard gave Norm an amused look. "Well, what did the man look like?" Willard asked. "Short or tall? Did he have a beard? How old do you think he was?"

Norm answered each question in great detail, and at that point I wondered which man, if either, was pulling the other's leg. Or were they both serious? After a while, Willard said, "You know, I think that was Ned Osborn. At least that's what I remember him looking like when I was a boy."

"Well, that's what I wondered," said Norm. And both men went quiet.

Louise and I were more than a bit curious and wanted more information. So Norm and Willard told us what they knew of the man who had built and lived in the house that the Dutchuks now owned.

Osborn was born in Kalmar, Sweden, and went to sea as a young boy, along with his good friend Charles Nelson. The two of them eventually wound up in Oysterville and settled next door to one another along Territory Road. Ned went to work as a sailmaker and, in 1873, began building a house for his bride-to-be.

Like many of the old homes in Oysterville, Osborn's house is a simple 'T' shape in plan, and the covered front porch, with its old-fashioned porch swing, is an inviting entryway to the house.

The front door opens directly into the kitchen. To the left is the parlor and the downstairs bedroom; to the right are the pantry and the bathroom. Along the rear wall, next to the kitchen sink and counter, a door opens onto a back porch. From the kitchen, a stairway leads to the large dormitory-style bedroom above—a room that can sleep as many as twelve.

Whether Ned intended to make separate bedrooms upstairs is unclear. As the house was nearing completion, he sent to the "old country" for his true love, but he learned that, tragically, she had recently died. Though he lived in the house for the rest of his days, Ned never married, nor did he finish the upstairs part of the house. Perhaps he had soured on life, Norm and Willard speculated. Perhaps that was why he didn't want people partying in his house into the wee hours.

By the time they had finished telling the tale, both Norm and Willard seemed convinced that the man who had come down those stairs the night before was Ned Osborn, even though he had been dead for more than fifty years. No one of us ever said the words "ghost" or "haunted" or "spirit." However, Ned Osborn became a "person of interest" in my mind, and when more information about him surfaced several years later, I was intrigued.

In 1978, I was cleaning out a closet in my

family's house when I ran across some notes on the back of an old envelope with a stamp cancellation date of 1947. In my grandfather's handwriting, almost like a poem, was new information about Ned and his house!

Ned Osborn House
1872 about
Built by Edward (Ned) Osborn
Batched there all his life
Died of stroke 1906
Alga Fagenstrom (?)
Engaged to & built house
For but engagement was broken.
He never married.
She died years later
Just before the upstairs
Was finished which was
Then never completed.
Wood—rough wood from South Bend
Finished lumber from California

The first thing that struck me was that Ned's sweetheart had apparently jilted him by choice, not through death. And that it wasn't until she married someone else that he gave up hope and stopped working on his house. It also sounded like she may have been a local girl, not a sweetheart left behind in Sweden.

But more astonishing to me than the "new" facts about Ned's intended was the date of Ned's death—four years before Willard was even born! There was no way Willard could have remembered Ned.

When I asked Willard about the dates, his eyes opened wide. "Really?" he said. "I'm absolutely sure I remember him!" And he said it so convincingly that I actually understood the feeling. Many are the stories that I have heard so many times that I truly believe I witnessed the events myself.

Norm and Willard remained friends for all the years they were neighbors in Oysterville.

Whether or not the two men ever discussed Ned Osborn's visit again, I don't know. Norm's son Mike reports that Ned never came downstairs again, but it was not uncommon to hear furniture being moved around upstairs even when all members of the household were present and accounted for . . . downstairs! Family and friends took for granted that it was Ned.

"All that stopped in the mid-eighties," says Mike. "Ned's wooden grave marker was getting pretty beat up at the cemetery, so Dad replaced it with a replica and brought the original here to the house for safe keeping. We have it in a protected area in the front yard. Ned, of course, is still up at the cemetery, but once his wooden marker came to the house, the upstairs noises stopped."

Or maybe, just maybe, Ned's ghost is glad to be reunited with his old wooden tombstone once again.

Oysterville Schoolhouse

The Ghost of Aunt Frances

Sally Sherwood and her twin sisters, Suzy and Kathy, were known as the three "good little girls." Not that they were perfect, but in the big, noisy Sherwood family, they always followed the one rule that no one else seemed to manage. Without fail and with no arguing, they went right upstairs when it was bedtime. That's because they shared a bedtime secret.

Every single night, they would wait for a visit with Aunt Frances. Actually, with her ghost. They saw Aunt Frances often, even though she had "gone to her reward" years before Sally and the twins were born. In truth, the "visits" were more like watching Aunt Frances and waiting for her to speak. But she never did.

Aunt Frances would arrive in a smoky-looking aura, and although she never identified herself, the girls knew exactly who she was. She was their mother's next oldest sister, Frances. Of their mother's ten brothers and sisters, Frances was the only one who had died.

When the sisters saw the ghost of their aunt, they were always just a little afraid. But not enough to get really spooked. Not enough to pull the covers over their heads or to run back downstairs where it was safe. They would lie in bed quietly until Aunt Frances would come and stand in the hallway, just outside their bedroom door. They thought that her room must have been the northeast bedroom, right across from theirs. And Aunt Frances visited them at bedtime as long as they slept upstairs in the old family house. When the girls moved to a downstairs bedroom, Aunt Frances no longer made her night visits.

Frances was born in 1909, the ninth child of Maggie and F.L. Sargant. Like many of the Sargant children, she went to Portland when she finished Ilwaco High School—the only secondary school on the Peninsula. In Portland, she lived with Mae, an older sister who already had a family of her own by then. In fact, it was Mae's ten-year-old daughter, Dorothy, who found Frances's body. Frances was in her late twenties, and she died under mysterious circumstances. That was back in 1934, and no one in the family ever talked about what happened—except when Dorothy once said that the body was all bloated and she could hardly tell it was Frances.

Sally and her sisters were born in the early 1940s and lived in the very same Oysterville farmhouse where her mother and Aunt Frances had grown up. The girls never could figure out why their aunt's ghost was hanging around their house, since she had died in Portland, Oregon, a full 120 miles away. Sally finally decided it must have been because Aunt Frances loved her childhood growing up in the big white house by the bay and going to the one-room school in Oysterville—just like Sally and the twins were doing all those years later.

When the twins were ten and Sally was almost twelve, the Sherwood family sold the farm and moved to California—everyone, that is, except for the ghost of Aunt Frances. According to the next few owners, the ghost stayed with the house for quite a while. Marilyn Casey, the second owner after the Sherwoods, still remembers a strange scent—like flowers—coming from that northeast

bedroom. And she says she never could keep that door shut. As tight as she closed it, it was always open six or eight inches when she went back upstairs.

Marilyn chose the downstairs bedroom for herself, but she soon began to hear footsteps overhead. Someone seemed to be walking in that northeast bedroom and out into the hall during the night. Marilyn was sure no one was up there. She didn't even go up to look. She just knew it was a ghost, and not a very scary one, either. Even so, she kept a weapon nearby . . . just in case.

In 1982, the Tom Downer family bought the house. Since then, none of that family—three generations of them—have seen or heard Aunt Frances. But a workman named Ron who was hired to do some remodeling has an interesting story to tell. He says that the first time he was aware of something odd going on was at the end of a long workday. He was taking some tools from the job site at the main house back to the old chicken shed where he kept his toolbox.

However, when he got there on that particular evening, his toolbox was gone. He looked everywhere on the property, even going back to the house to see if he'd taken it there and forgotten. No toolbox. But, a few hours later, when he checked the chicken shed again, there it was! Right in the middle of the floor! Nothing was disturbed or missing. The toolbox was just sitting there!

When Ron learned, some months later, that there was supposed to be a ghost in the house, he was disappointed that he had never seen it. Soon, though, strange things began happening

at his own house! Nothing really bad, just mischievous antics like borrowing the car keys—things a teenager might do, Ron remembers. But the ghost never showed herself or did anything when he was working on Tom's house except for "borrowing" his toolbox that time. Since Tom says the ghost has never been seen by his family, Ron is pretty sure that's because she's over at his place in Ocean Park now!

Mysterious Tragedy at Sprague's Hole

Sprague's Hole was one of those wonderful swampy places where kids love to fool around— the kind of places that were common on the Peninsula before dikes and drainage ditches dried things out. It was where boys hunted pollywogs or kept an eye on a beaver dam or went to check on those mallard ducklings that hatched last week. Sprague's Hole was located somewhere between Ocean Park and Nahcotta. Nowadays, no one can remember just where.

"Three Bright School Boys Meet Death in Sprague's Hole" said the headline in the Ilwaco Tribune. It happened on a Thursday in April 1912. Victor Slingerland and Lester Young, both twelve years old, and Phillip Brooks, ten, drowned on their way home from school in Nahcotta. No one ever knew for sure, but it was thought that they had stopped at Sprague's Hole to pick up the snipe Lester's older brother had shot that morning.

Maybe they had taken time to row that old boat out to the deepest part, and somehow, they capsized. It was said that Phillip and Victor probably drowned at once. Their bodies were found at the bottom of the pond by Victor's dad. Somehow, Lester had managed to reach the shore, too exhausted to drag himself farther. He died there hours before the tragedy was discovered.

A funeral for all three boys was held on Sunday in the Methodist chapel in Ocean Park. The entire community attended, and there was standing room only. There was no school on Monday "out of respect for the families," the county school superintendent said.

It took a long, long time, but gradually life got back to normal. And now, most people have forgotten. They have forgotten the tragedy and the names of the boys. They have forgotten that the Brooks house was once rented to families named Venable and Asanuma. They have forgotten that the Wiegardts bought it and later rented it to oystermen and their families.

And they have forgotten that Phillip Brooks's friend Victor Slingerland had a sister named Beulah who married Ed Wickberg. Beulah and Ed's daughter Lucille Wickberg Wilson began the Ark Restaurant—the very restaurant that Jimella Lucas and Nanci Main owned when the Brooks house caught Nanci's attention.

"I wasn't even intending to buy a house," says Nanci. "I was driving by and saw the 'For Sale' sign. The house seemed to call to me." That was in 1985. Nanci had never heard of the Brooks family or of Sprague's Hole or of the terrible tragedy that had involved young Phillip Brooks and his friends.

"At that time," says Nanci, "the house was known in the community as the 'Wiegardt House' and there was a 'W' on the gate. The 'W' has long since fallen off, but I've kept the gate, even though I had to replace the fence itself. To me, the gate is another community connection.

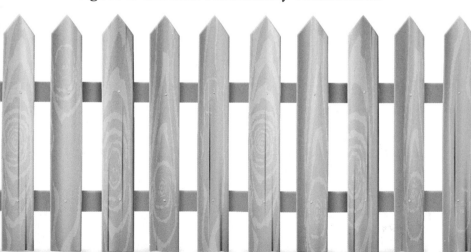

"From the time I moved in, people were so generous in sharing their memories about the house and its place in their lives. My neighbor Ed Chellis told me that he remembered going to the Brooks house when he was a boy to see someone who had been 'laid out.' That was common in those days—to have the viewing of the body in the living room of the house where the dead person had lived. I imagine it was Mrs. Brooks whom he was paying his respects to.

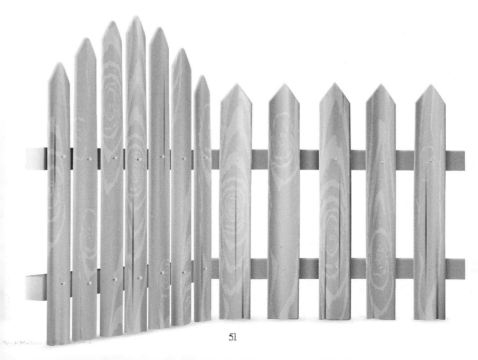

"Even the siren at the fire hall across the way has seemed friendly. I once lived in a house that burned to the ground. I lost everything—dishes, photographs, mementos from the past. So, when I hear the siren go at night and then within minutes hear the firemen going off in the fire rigs, I feel a great sense of comfort and gratitude.

"My house is such a loving, generous-spirited house. I know it has many stories to tell, if only it could," says Nanci.

"But there is one room that is much different from all the others. It's the upstairs back bedroom. There is a stillness there. A sort of quiet waiting. I'm sure it must have been young Phillip's room.

"Another thing—despite the sturdiness of the house, even during big storms—there are often times that doors, especially the trapdoor to the attic, mysteriously open. It's as if someone has entered or left but has neglected to shut the door behind them. Much like a ten-year-old boy might do!

"Not long after I moved in, a friend—a psychic friend—came to visit me. No sooner had she walked in the door than she said to me, 'There are thirteen spirits in this house.'"

Nanci says she has never actually seen any of the spirits in the house. But she is well aware of their nearness. "Sometimes I'll catch a movement out of the corner of my eye, but when I turn to look, there is nothing unusual there. And many, many times I have felt an icy draft of air; yet my house is always warm and airtight—there are no drafty places. It's always a comforting energy—never terrifying or blood-curdling.

"Not all ghosts are scary, you know," says Nanci. "The thirteen in my house couldn't be friendlier—most of the time!"

The Ghost Ship Solano

It's been more than sixty years since the *Solano* has made an appearance on the Long Beach Peninsula. Only the oldest generation remembers seeing the ancient ship's rotting hull sitting high and dry on the beach. Not since the 1960s has anyone been able to walk right up to her, climb aboard her, and explore her remains. They still talk about her, though. They simply call her "the Wreck" or "the Ghost Ship," and they know she will be back.

The *Solano* was a 728-ton, four-masted American schooner sailing north past the Long Beach Peninsula on her way from San Francisco to Grays Harbor when she ran into trouble. It was February 5, 1905, still a time when the tall ships sailed the seas of the world and long before radar and other aids to navigation had been invented to help keep ships and sailors safe. Luckily for

the *Solano*, the lookout at the life-saving station south of Ocean Park saw her distress signal through his telescope and sounded the alarm.

Immediately, the life-saving crew gathered up equipment and made its way north along the sandy shore. Although the tide was very high, the surf was unusually calm for a winter day, and the surfmen were able to get the shipwrecked seamen ashore with little difficulty. (Even a small dog was rescued from the unlucky ship.) On close inspection at low tide, the schooner was found to be undamaged, so plans were made to refloat her.

However, ten long months would go by before a tide would be high enough to relaunch the ship. Meanwhile, the captain and crew continued to live aboard the landlocked vessel. Visitors to the area were astonished to see the sailing ship, fully upright, far from the water and completely surrounded by the sands of the broad ocean beach, often with the crew's clean laundry flapping from the rigging. On the other hand, the county wreckmaster, whose job it was to protect shipwrecks from souvenir hunters (called "seagulls" by local residents), seldom felt it necessary to visit the *Solano* at all.

As the months went by, the crew worked tirelessly to prepare the vessel for relaunching. On the highest tide of December 1907, the task was successfully completed. Arrangements had been made with the owners of the tugboat *Daring* to be there at the time of the schooner's refloating so that she could be towed safely to port. All went according to schedule except... the tugboat never showed up!

As the *Solano* floated helplessly, a strong south wind whipped up a rough surf. Hour by hour, the breakers increased in fury until, finally, they drove the ship back onto the beach not far from where she had waited so patiently to be rescued. This time, any further attempts to save the ship were abandoned. For years, the Solano sat on the beach just south of Oysterville, gradually disintegrating in the turbulent coastal weather, until it became hard to imagine that the gnarled old hull that remained had once been a proud sailing ship.

As time passed, even the *Solano's* hull began to sink into the sand. Some years it would disappear altogether, only to resurface for a few more seasons. People began to refer to her as "the Ghost Ship," and by the mid-1920s, everyone thought she had vanished for good. However, in 1933, the sands shifted drastically once more. Again, the hull became visible, and for the next four decades, the old wreck stubbornly refused to be reburied.

As the years passed, weather bleached her wooden hull white, and barnacles encased her, her appearance became more and more ghostly. Even though she was considered unsafe to walk on, the big Dungeness crabs that lived in the tidepools below her deck were too great a temptation for locals. With buckets and garden rakes, they would risk climbing onto the rotting hull to capture the seafood delicacies for their family dinner tables.

Children, especially, found the old wreck irresistible. Gary Whitlow, who grew up in Oysterville, often talks about going out to the *Solano* with his friends. They would hike down the beach at low tide, carefully climb up onto what remained of the deck, and wait there until the tide came in deep enough for fishing. By then, of course, the water was surrounding them, and they would have to wait, sometimes for hours, until the tide went out enough to get off the slippery, rotting deck.

But in the mid-1960s, the wreck disappeared again. As the years have gone by, people have begun to forget its exact location. The dunes continue to shift and grow, and the once-familiar landmarks have changed. Newcomers to the Peninsula are amazed to learn that the landlocked wreck ever existed and that the cars on the Ocean Beach Highway might actually be driving right over the bones of an old ship.

However, the folks who remember the Solano still keep a sharp lookout for her ghostly white hull. They are confident that she will rise again to share her secrets with those who are brave enough to listen. "She'll be back," say the old-timers. "The Ghost Ship *Solano* will be back!"

CHAPTER 7

A House Fit for a Bride

Peninsula people call it "the Wedding Cake House." The white, three-storied building topped with a widow's walk not only looks like a gigantic wedding cake, but it was also built for Elizabeth Lambert Wood in 1894 as a wedding present when she married Dr. William Wood.

No one remembers whether the seventeen-room house was a gift from her father or from her husband. What folks do remember are the many tragedies Mrs. Wood endured during the long years she owned the house. The young couple's main residence was in Portland, but they spent their summers in the Long Beach house.

Things began to go badly not long after their wedding, when William became ill with tuberculosis. In 1901, the couple and their two young children, Lambert and Helen, moved to Arizona hoping that a drier and hotter climate would help William recuperate. After a few years, Dr. Wood's health improved, and the family moved back to the Northwest. However, they returned to Oracle each winter. No matter where they lived, their summer place in Long Beach remained a constant.

But before long, Mrs. Wood's life took a devastating turn. Lambert was killed in France in July 1918 during World War I. In 1923, after several years of declining health, her beloved husband also died. About that same time, Helen's marriage ended, and she moved back to Long Beach with her young son.

For reasons known only to the family, Mrs. Wood soon adopted Helen's son, then four years old, to raise as her own, even renaming him Lambert. Less than a year later, while on a vacation voyage, Helen was lost overboard in the Indian Ocean.

In the years that followed, Elizabeth Wood spent more time in Long Beach devoting herself to her grandson Lambert and pursuing her two great interests—writing children's books and teaching Sunday school. After graduating from Ilwaco High School in 1938, Lambert went to the University of Arizona. When World War II began, he joined the Army Air Forces. Then, in a cruel twist of fate, he was killed when his fighter plane crashed in Texas—the second of Mrs. Wood's Lamberts to be lost during a world war.

Despite the many tragedies in her life, Mrs. Wood continued to write and do good works on Long Beach Peninsula. She donated acres of land to the Lone Fir Cemetery, saw to it that a library was started at the Long Beach Grammar School, and gave generously to several Peninsula churches. She died in 1962 a beloved member of the Peninsula community.

Mrs. Elizabeth Wood had been dead ten years before Candy and Frank Glenn III purchased the lovely old house. By then, it no longer sat alone a mile north of Long Beach. Nor was it at the very edge of the high tide line. By 1972, the town had built up around the house, and the beach sands stretched out in front of it by almost half a mile—a perfect playground for their daughter, Erin, and for Sonny, who was born a short time later.

Though all four of the Glenns are very sentimental about their time in the house, not all of them have the same thoughts about the "spirit" of the house. Frank, for instance, says flat out that he never had the feeling that there was any kind of "presence" or ghost in the house at all.

Candy, on the other hand, says, "The minute you enter the house you feel a wonderful, warm embrace of welcome. But it is in her third-floor writing studio that I feel Mrs. Wood's presence the most. Her typewriter still sits on the desk up there. There is no doubt in my mind that Mrs. Wood's spirit is here and that she is thankful that we are caring for her beloved house."

"For me, there has always been an air of magic about the house," says Erin. She moved back into the house as an adult and vividly recalls the experience she had on one of the first nights she was there. "I was asleep, and a large, older woman approached and leaned over my bed. She was carrying a tray of offerings—different sorts of objects and figurines. It wasn't like a dream. I felt it was real—like it was actually happening. I knew, absolutely, that the woman was Mrs. Wood and that she was greeting me and receiving me back into the house. She was presenting me with gifts of welcome."

Only Sonny has had really scary experiences in the house. "But," he insists, "I love the house. There's just one room I'm actually afraid of. I call it the 'Cranberry Room.' It's the southeast bedroom—always a guest room since our family has had the house. I had a really bad experience there when I was about seven years old.

"I was home alone one afternoon listening to records in that room when suddenly I felt I was not alone. I didn't actually see anyone—at least no earthly person was there. It just began to feel heavy and stifling in there, and I wanted to run out. After that, I stayed far away from that room. I felt as if someone or something might unexpectedly come out of it."

Sonny moved back into the house for a time when he was an adult. "I was sleeping in the room that I think was Helen's room," says Sonny. "There is some mystery about her death. Like did she fall overboard? Or did she jump? Whatever the story is, that particular room just isn't cheerful. There is a troubled presence there. It's not like the rest of the house.

"One night as I lay in bed, in the dark, eyes wide open, the air began to become dense; I could actually feel it thickening. As I watched, a misty shape wafted in. Soon it looked like an aged, wizened woman, and her head was floating toward me! She was so very old—like 150 years old. I finally had to pull the covers over my head!"

Sonny feels sure that the evil-feeling presence is Helen, but he is not certain what her unhappiness is all about. "Mostly, I have a good feeling in the house. Many of the rooms feel like the restful places you would expect to find in a seaside home. Mrs. Wood's presence is positive but does not wipe away the feeling of Helen's discontent, which seems centered in that Cranberry Room."

These days, Erin and her fourteen-year-old son Diego live in the house, and the strange activity has settled down. Mostly. Though Erin sometimes "gets a strange feeling" in the kitchen, Diego has never seen or felt a thing. Their dog Blueberry, though, is another story. "She often sees things the rest of us can't see. I wish she could tell us about who and what she sees in our house!" says Erin. "I think we would be amazed!"

Why does Helen hang out in this house where she was so unhappy? And what about Mrs. Wood? Is she waiting for her two Lamberts to come back home? Maybe Blueberry knows the answers . . .

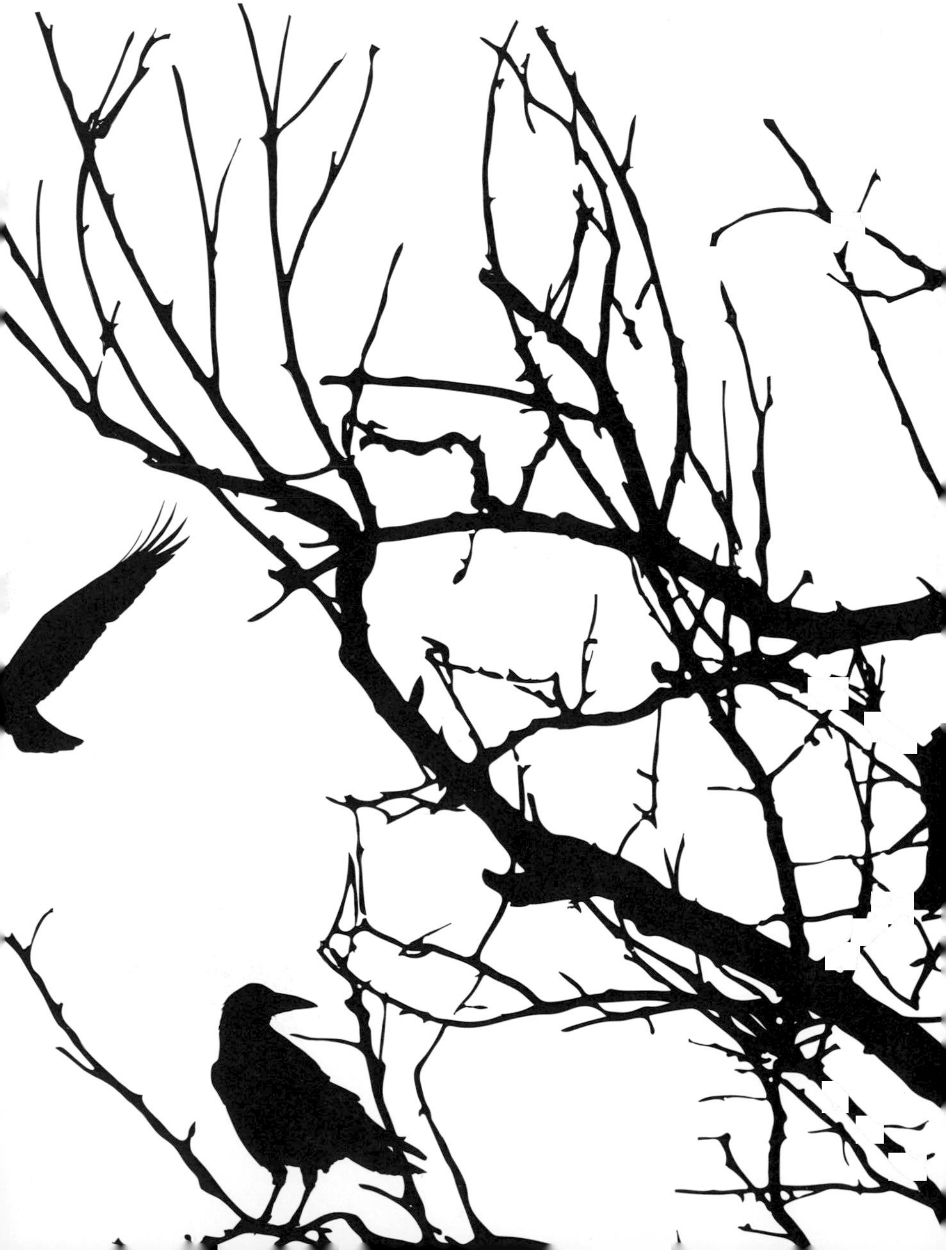

CHAPTER 8

The Little Girl at the Manor

"Who's the little girl?" Roy's friend asked him. Roy Gustafson looked around the room. There was no one else there. Only the two of them. There was a party going on in the other rooms nearby to celebrate the completed remodel of the beautiful old house. But all the guests were adults, friends of Roy and his partner, Gordon. No children had been invited.

"She was here for only a minute," the friend said. "Five or six years old, dressed all in white. I thought she might belong to one of your guests."

"She didn't by any chance have a cat with her, did she?" The answer was "no" and the men rejoined the party. But afterward, Roy and Gordon discussed what Roy's friend had seen; they both knew. Even though she didn't have her ghost cat with her, they knew it was the little girl ghost from upstairs. It was the only time in the twenty-two years they owned the house that anyone had actually seen her. But she was often heard.

The big house on Twelfth and South Idaho Streets is a landmark in Long Beach. For more than one hundred years, it has dominated the block on which it stands, looking as though it has many stories to tell. Oh, if only it could talk!

Originally a farmhouse, the Manor was built in 1893 on the edge of a big swamp. By the time Gordon and Roy bought the place, it contained many small rooms. "Perhaps," they were told, "after its use as a farmhouse, the building had been a hotel or maybe a hospital or a home for young girls."

Although they didn't know much about the Manor's history, they did suspect from the minute they moved in that the house was haunted. "There

was just an odd feeling in the house, especially upstairs." However, it wasn't until they had finished some remodeling projects that the two men began to hear the noises. And every time, they would make their way up the steep, narrow stairs and go to check.

There was never anyone there, nothing had moved or fallen, and there wasn't a logical explanation. As time went by, the noises became

more defined. Fast, light footsteps, like those a child might make, could clearly be heard. Sometimes it seemed that a small animal was with the child.

"We'd always had cats and we knew cat sounds. The animal we heard was definitely a cat," Roy says. "In the beginning, we would assume it was our Chessie. But when we glanced around, we'd see Chessie sound asleep on her favorite pillow or sometimes one of us would actually be holding her! So, upstairs we would go to see if, by chance, some other animal had gotten in. I had visions of a big rat," he laughs, "but we never found anything. Gradually it got so we simply assumed it was the ghost child's cat. If Chessie heard the same noises we did, she never gave any indication."

They mostly heard the noises while sitting in their living room, which was situated in the addition directly below the upstairs hallway. And the child seemed most active while guests were present, though no one ever saw her except that one time.

But that wasn't the only time that the little girl ghost did more than make noise. When Greta McDougall was house- and cat-sitting one summer, she was awakened by the sensation that something had landed on her bed. She had been warned that she might hear unexplained noises, but she was not prepared for this.

Immediately wide awake, she got up and walked quietly around the upstairs but heard nothing and saw nothing . . . until she returned to her room. The end of the bed was moving up and down as if a child were bouncing on the bed. Perhaps as a throwback to her own childhood when bed-bouncing was forbidden, she said in a stern voice, "Stop that! Stop right now." And the bouncing stopped.

Greta had one other experience with what folks came to think of as the "naughty little girl." One night, she was awakened by the sound of the drawer on the bedside stand opening and shutting, opening and shutting. Not only was it annoying, but she later said it felt like it was being done deliberately. Again, she spoke sternly, and again, the naughty behavior stopped.

Even more alarming than the noises was the smell of smoke. Several times Gordon and Roy rushed upstairs looking for a possible fire. "We were always aware of living in a big wooden house, and fire was a concern. More than once, we would get the strong odor of smoke and, as we frantically searched, it seemed that the smell became stronger as we went upstairs. But we never found anything," Roy says.

According to Gordon, "There was one dreadful story that might have explained the connection between the old house, the little girl, and the smoky smell. A neighbor said there once was a young girl associated with our property—maybe related to the owners—who had died in a bonfire accident on the beach."

Several years before Gordon and Roy moved from the Manor, the haunting stopped. No more noises from upstairs. No more unexplained smell of smoke. The little girl and her cat were gone. "You know," Gordon says with a smile, "we almost missed them."

The Shelburne

CHAPTER 9

The Man Upstairs
at the Shelburne

The Shelburne Inn in Seaview has been open longer than any other hotel in Washington, so it's no wonder that it has a ghost or two. One mysterious man upstairs was bothering guests, and owner David Campiche wanted him gone!

David, who has owned the Shelburne since 1977, had put up with that ghost from day one. "We were beginning some major renovations and were all busy in the dining room when we heard

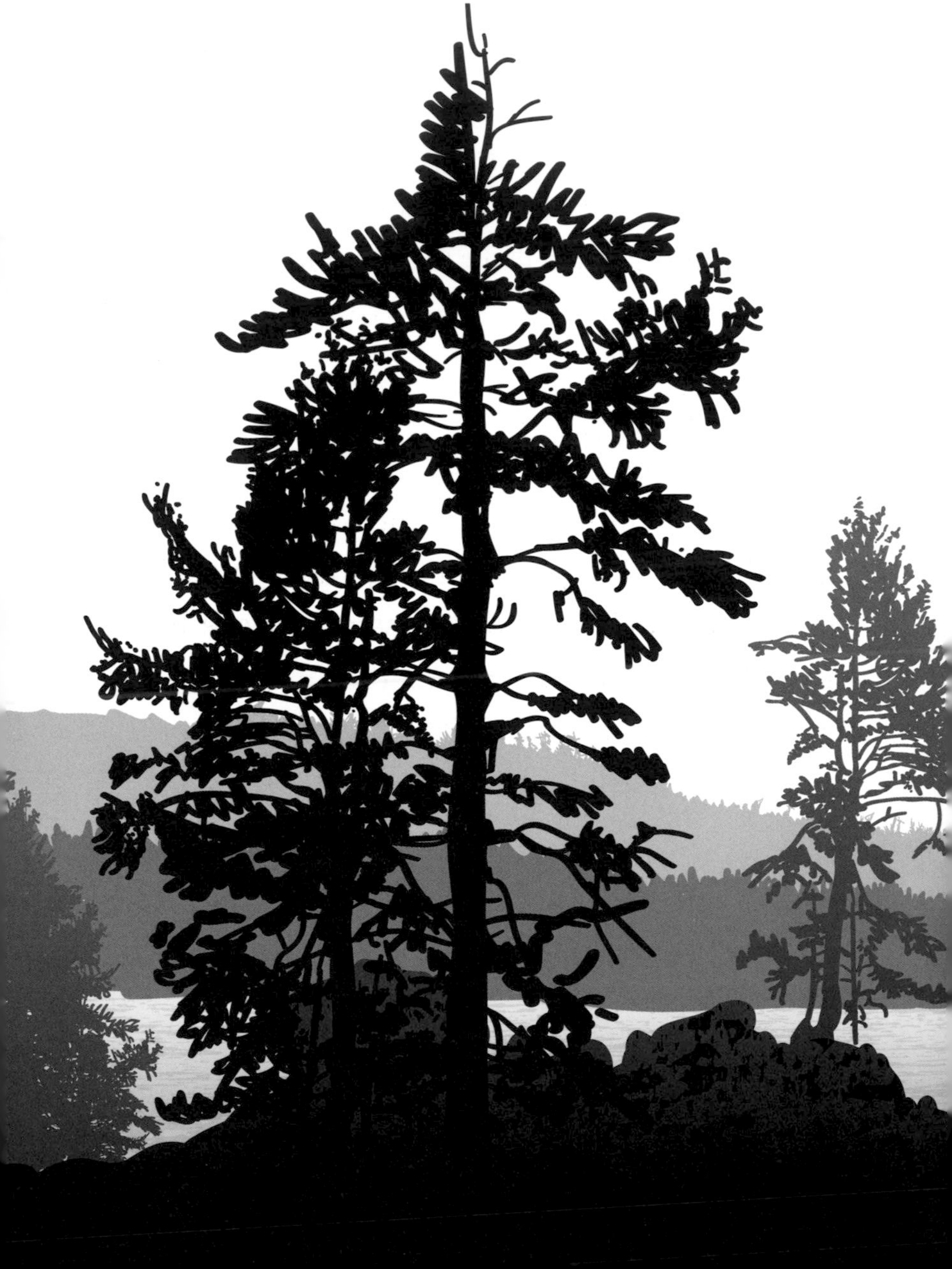

someone going up the back stairs. I remember being annoyed that someone had come in the building and gone upstairs without even asking."

When they heard a man's footsteps from up on the third floor, David went to take a look. "There was no one there—no evidence that anyone had been up there at all. It was our first inkling that perhaps we had a ghost."

As the years passed, that inkling grew to an absolute certainty. Although neither David nor his wife, Laurie, ever saw the ghost, overnight guests often did. One woman said that she had met an elderly gentleman in the upstairs hall who asked her to sit at Table 9 in the dining room—the table at the bottom of the back stairs.

He wanted to stand at the top and watch her eat. "Creepy as it was, she agreed," says David. "We all assumed he was watching her, though he didn't show himself to any of us, not even to her."

David often felt an icy, dense patch of air in that upstairs hallway and heard noises that no one could explain. "It's right where the old and new parts of the building meet, so in a way, it made sense that a ghost might hang out there."

That old part of the inn was built in 1896 as a hotel and boardinghouse and was located across the street from the present-day Shelburne. It was two-and-a-half stories and had fourteen rooms for permanent and summer guests, plus living quarters for builder Charles L. Beaver, his wife, Inez, and their two young children, Harold and Faye. Charles put Inez in charge of it while he was busy with his own career as a building contractor.

The Beavers ran the Shelburne for ten years before selling it to Timothy and Julia Hoare. The Hoares soon enlarged the hotel, though not in the usual way. Across the street from the Shelburne was property with two houses on it and room on the lot for a third building. Timothy bought the property, hired a team of horses to pull the hotel across the street, and placed it at the north end, in line with the other two buildings. A covered passageway was built between each of the buildings, joining them together and making a much larger hotel.

When Timothy Hoare died in 1921, Julia ran the hotel alone until her own death in 1939. Julia's second-floor room was number 8, just above the front door. From her window, she could keep an eye on the comings and goings of her guests and the hired help. It is in Room 8 that one of the strangest of the ghostly happenings occurred.

"A man from California was staying in that room and he got locked out," says David. "Besides the lock, which required a key, and which the man had kept with him, there was a deadbolt on the door that could only be locked or unlocked from the inside. This man locked his room from the outside with the key, left the hotel for a time, and when he returned, found that, although his key worked fine, the room remained locked from the inside. Someone had locked the deadbolt!"

David to the rescue! "I had to crawl out the window of the room next door, inch my way along the porch roof, jimmy open Room 8's window, and crawl inside to unlock the deadbolt. Not long after that, we replaced the deadbolt lock and never had that trouble again."

But the mysterious noises, the cold air in the hallway, and other weird things continued. A psychic brought a group of people to the inn for a few days. When they checked in, the psychic said to me, "I know who your ghost is." I was intrigued. We had never discussed the ghost at all. I didn't realize she knew anything about it. "He is Charles Beaver," she said.

"If it was Charles Beaver, was he upset that his hotel had been moved across the street? Or maybe he didn't like it being joined to another house," says David. "It is interesting that it was Julia Hoare's room that he locked. Was he locking her out?"

When the psychic asked David if he wanted the ghost to go away, he didn't hesitate. " 'Yes,' I said! And four or five days later she telephoned me." She said he was gone. She saw him leave with two angels.

Since then, all ghost activity at the Shelburne has stopped. For now.

North Head Lighthouse

The
Lightkeeper's Wife

Mary Pesonen had put in twenty-five long years as the lightkeeper's wife at North Head Lighthouse, which overlooked the Pacific Ocean just north of Cape Disappointment. For all that time, she had endured loneliness and isolation on the high cliff at the end of the Peninsula. She had endured the gales of winter and the endless days of murky fog and relentless rain. She had cooked and cleaned, cared for the animals, and tended the gardens.

And she had recently received a clean bill of health from her doctor in Portland.

So why, on the morning of June 9, 1923, did she choose to end her life? Or did she?

The Ilwaco Tribune reported: "Her death occurred last Saturday morning when she threw herself over the towering cliffs at North Head and dashed herself to death on the jagged rocks below." But is that really what happened?

According to Mary's husband, Alexander, she had seemed especially cheerful the previous evening. Just that day, he had brought her home from Portland, where she had been recovering from a bout of "melancholia," as depression was then called. "It was good to see Mary cheerful again after being down in the dumps for so long," Alexander Pesonen said.

On Saturday morning, she got up at five o'clock, telling her husband to stay in bed for a bit. She was going to do some errands and take a walk, as was her custom, plus it was an activity advised by her doctor. A short while later, the dog, always a companion on her walks, returned . . . but Mary did not. It was the "queer antics" of the dog that alerted Alex to the possibility of trouble.

The news report stated: "A searching party was soon organized. The dog led searchers to a spot near the North Head lighthouse, and there they found her coat lying on the edge of the cliff. A trail through the tall grass, as though someone had slid down the cliff was mute evidence of what had befallen the unfortunate woman. About five o'clock in the evening, the body was found lying in a little cove just beyond the Pesonen garden, where it had drifted with the tide."

Why Mary chose that particular Saturday to end her life was a question Alex could never answer. They had been planning on his retirement in just six months. They were looking forward to moving to land they owned near Shoalwater Bay—land where they would grow cranberries. And they would spend their winters in California. "I thought she was looking forward to it," said her heartbroken husband.

There wasn't much known about Mary Pesonen. Only that her maiden name was Watson, that she was fifty-three years old, a native of Ireland, and that she and Alex had been married for twenty-seven years. They had no children.

Alexander K. Pesonen was the first lightkeeper at North Head, beginning there on the day the light was put into service on May 16, 1898. He and Mary moved into the keeper's residence, also newly constructed, as were the barn and outbuildings on the property.

The lightkeeper's main duty was to make sure that the light operated each night between sunset and sunrise. By day, he scoured and polished the glass prisms of the light, and by night, he tended the burning oil. It required a degree of physical strength and consistent attention, but mostly, it was a repetitive, monotonous job for which he was paid about $800 per year. These duties were clearly laid out, and regular inspections were held. The work of wives was also inspected, even though they were not paid for their work. How well they did their tasks was reflected in the ratings of their husband.

In those years before electricity and running water, there was an enormous amount of work involved in maintaining a household on the stormy cliffs of North Head. Besides the usual cooking, cleaning, sewing, and other household chores, Mary also cleaned the outhouse, kept the sheds, stables, and grounds neatly maintained, and cared for the garden and the animals, which probably included chickens, a cow, and several horses, at the very least. For a woman who suffered from bouts of melancholia, the responsibilities may have seemed overwhelming.

The North Head Light is now fully automatic, and the house where Mary and Alexander Pesonen lived is called the Lighthouse Keeper's Residence and is a vacation rental at Cape Disappointment

State Park. Years went by after Mary's death before the first "disturbances" at the lighthouse keeper's residence were reported.

If those who stay there are to be believed, the house has more to offer than three bedrooms and an updated kitchen with modern conveniences. The lightkeeper's house also comes with a ghost! Renters tell of strange activities in the house and on the grounds—blinking lights, mysterious

electrical disturbances, and a shadowy figure who wanders around outside. Is it the ghost of Mary Pesonen?

There are still many questions about what really happened on that long-ago Saturday morning. Did Mary Pesonen slip and fall? Or perhaps she tripped over the dog? Or did

someone push her? And are the disturbances Mary's way of trying to tell her story?

Just like the fog that shrouds the nearby cliffs of Cape Disappointment, mystery clings to Mary Pesonen, the lightkeeper's wife. So far, her story is incomplete. Will we ever know how she ended up on the rocks at the bottom of the cliff? Or is it only the crashing waves and screaming seagulls who have the answers?

Author and historian **Sydney Stevens**, herself a local legend, is a fourth-generation Oysterville resident. During her 39-year career as an elementary teacher, she wrote social studies texts and local history books. She has devoted herself to the research and publication of regional history, especially the stories of previous generations.

Check out some of the other Spooky America titles available now!

Spooky America was adapted from the creeptastic Haunted America series for adults. Haunted America explores historical haunts in cities and regions across America. Each book chronicles both the widely known and less-familiar history behind local ghosts and other unexplained mysteries. Here are more from *Ghost Stories of the Long Beach Peninsula* author Sydney Stevens:

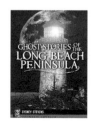
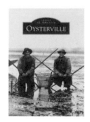